Steve Martland

Skywalk
(1989)

for five solo voices or mixed chorus (SSATB)

ED 12362

SCHOTT

Mainz · London · Madrid · New York · Paris · Prag · Tokyo · Toronto

This is a new edition of a work that was originally published in 1989.

First Performance: 24 June 1989
                     Nantwich Choral Society
                     Stephen Buckman, conductor
                     St. Mary's Church, Nantwich

Duration: c. 8 minutes

Skywalk

I see the horizon,
A light blue, a blue band.
This is the Earth, how beautiful she is!
Everything is fine!

I see a vision
of divinity, God's Earth,
the scars of national boundaries gone!
Everything is fine!

Minerva breathes,
Apollo guides me,
A long way to go, just to check the view!
Everything is fine!

I am the eagle
on the rock and
look! by holding up my thumb
I blot the Earth from the Universe!
Everything is fine!

A single eye of blue
that gazed on space
is changing to another hue
the Face itself looks on the Face
unfolding time
the final gyre – gives out.

Skywalk

Stevan Keane

Steve Martland

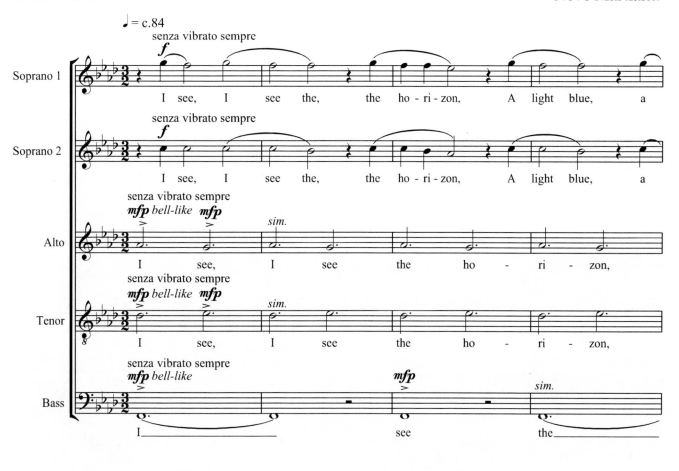

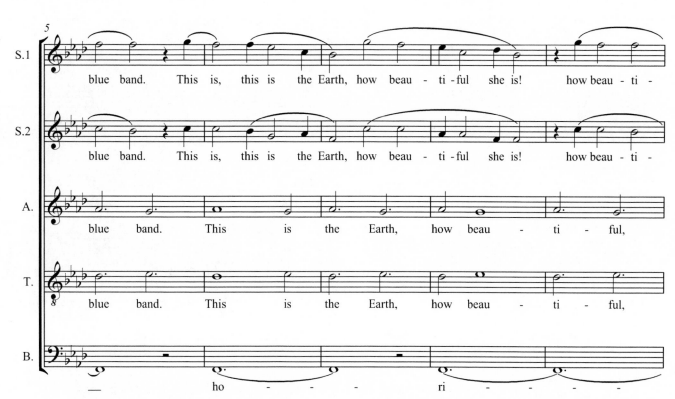

2

4

6

Schott & Co. Ltd, London S&Co.8006